C000177808

SEAHENGE: A JOURNEY

Text © Kevin Crossley-Holland 2019
Images © Andrew Rafferty 2019
All rights reserved

First published by Kailpot Press in 2019
11 Horsecroft Road,
Hemel Hempstead,
Hertfordshire,
HP1 1PZ

The rights of Kevin Crossley-Holland
and Andrew Rafferty to be identified
as the Authors of this work has been
asserted by them in accordance with
the Copyrights, Designs and Patents
Act 1988.

No part of this book may be reprinted
or reproduced or utilised in any form
or by any electronic, mechanical or
other means, now known or hereafter
invented, including photocopying
and recording, or in any information
storage or retrieval system, without the
permission in writing from the Publisher.

British Library
Cataloguing-in-Publication Data

A catalogue record for this book is
available from the British Library.

ISBN 978-0-9556860-4-7

Designed by Kailpot Press
Printed by Gutenberg Press, Malta

ACKNOWLEDGEMENTS

Very many thanks for their expertise and encouragement to:

Peter Abbs
Karen Clarke
Rachel Gibson
Mick Gowar
Amanda Loose
Rowan Mantell
Simon Millward
Chris Rafferty
Pete Rafferty
Jim Ring
Stephen Stuart-Smith
Dina Thorpe

and to our wives, Linda and Alison.

Kevin Crossley-Holland & Andrew Rafferty

SEAHENGE: A JOURNEY

KEVIN CROSSLEY-HOLLAND & ANDREW RAFFERTY

KAILPOT PRESS

CONTENTS

SEAHENGE: A JOURNEY

TUMP

Back again! Back
and up to that oval tump above the chalk cross
to search for a thumbnail of pottery,
a single sherd.
When I launched myself into the trench beside it,
packed with crackling beech-leaves,
I believed I was an inmate of the barrow.

Commentator, diplomat, viola player, priest
– all four beached on my limitations
and quickening sense of myself.
But why did I not train to be an archaeologist?

That riddled oak lectern,
and the scarabs and beads from Ur,
a nacreous perfume bottle lifted
from some settlement south of Alexandria...
Asking, deducing, dovetailing
past and present, matter and spirit:

my heart quickens
to Whiteleaf and my childhood museum,
that shed growing into the ground,

and with one eye on the threatening sky,
one on a molehill,
I brighten at the little finds
I'm still adding to it.

DEADHEADED

Undone, a necklace of rose lights
looping over the Chilterns
above the spring line
(no culture chooses to look down at its dead)
then on through the wilderness of this world
– the airy Downs, silly Suffolk –
each blossom radiant, fading,
deadheaded.

Sky widens, and the chain tautens.
Footfalls in the sandy soil and soggy fen,

footfalls through forests bedded
with cones and needles:

knappers and salt-panners and oyster-men,
truth-tellers, outcasts, devotees
still resting here.

Sudden gusts and bluster,
bolts of thunder, stinging rain,
and no less sudden,
wings of Chalk Hill blues again.

High over the henge and all its voices
there's a spray of lights, a cluster:
shoulder-companions on this last ridge
at the end of their long journey
– dark roses before the drop
to the baffled sea.

UNLIVING

With mommets and hodmedods
we tried to scare him away.
For a while we did.
Death flew off with his demons
and you burned brightly.

When we propped you
against the door-post
you heard your willow-daughter
comforting her daughter
who will soon be born.

You kept begging us
to call on our ancestors.
Flame-cheeks, twitch-fingers.
You kept saying the unliving
can guard the living.

SHIMMER

All day you waited
outside your hut,
not alone,

and murmured and warbled
last words
before you lost your breath.

You watched how the ridge
grew holy
and how the end of the evening
shimmered
the bristling fields
copper and bronze

even your own messengers
the waves of the sky
no longer mud-foul
but oyster and pearl

while sea–eagles and harriers
before their bloody work
made low passes

TREE

When you came I was unborn.

No one knew your name
or where you had walked from.
'Along the living streams,' you said.

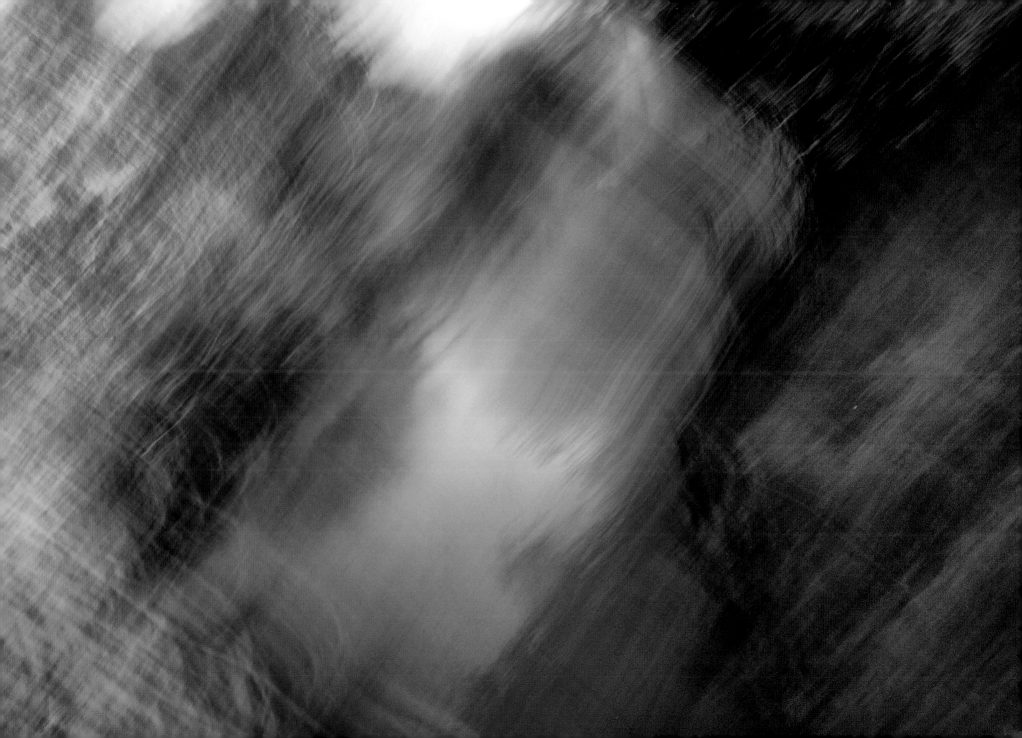

You told us there's a tree
opening over all that is
            all that is
– white skull, green earth, swarming sea.
'It sings and suffers for us.
It is our always tree.'

You said when our leader dies,
each of us is turned over, each is broken.
You told us to smash all the death-urns
and nick the axe-blades
to set their spirits free,
then lay him in the cradle
of an upturned tree.

'Do this,' you said,
'and he will be sky-born again.
After the fire and flood
you too will be sky-born again.'

Our grandfathers and great grandmothers
laughed they cried
and in the rush-light
they asked you many questions.

I know I would have seen you
before sunrise
up there on the lopeway
just below the ridge.

ALTAR

I closed your lids
with this right thumb.
Then we fashioned your death-cradle.
The elders and the lame
with chains of song unbroken,
and the young splashing, delving, squeezing out,
then heaping up your island,
all the men and women with their singing axes.

With honeysuckle ropes we snared the posts
and set them up in trenches side by side.
Past the hazels and alders
we hauled the huge oak-stump
with its horn roots to the bog.
We chipped all the bark
from your cradle.
   Your white altar.
   Your shining altar.

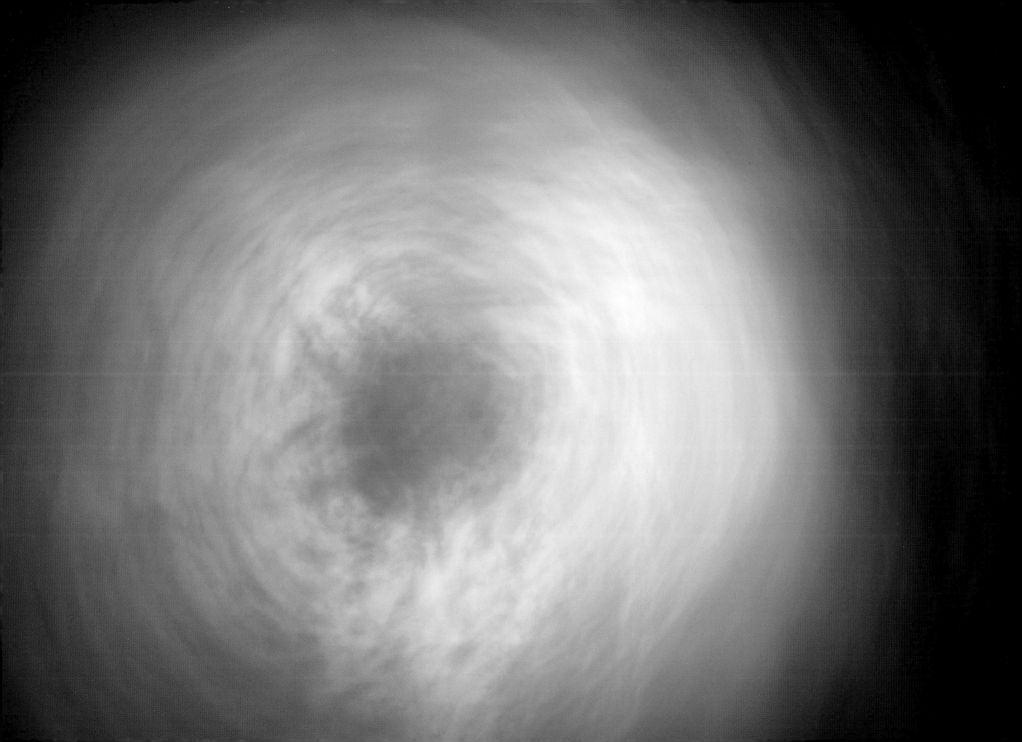

From where sun dies the wind blew,
tides gulped and shunted
behind our dunes for many days.
But at last we lifted you
on thick green trusses and silver wormwood
we carried you out from the dead-house.

You wore flowers.
You wore flowers.
Sun-cups, silken cottongrass,
threaded and twisted,
starlight, marsh-mallow.
Your choker wreathen sea-pink.

So gently we laid you
on the crush of chalk and clay
between the roots
of the upturned tree.
        Our death-baby.
        Our death-baby.

Each of us sipped three sips
of the sweet water, the sweet water
lapping you.
And I, blood of your blood,
placed your death-gifts around you.

The sea-eagles and harriers heard our cries.
They cried with us.

Then each of us sang.
I sang I felt the darkness knotting
inside you.
I sang you were the setting sun.
I sang until I closed the lids
over your eyes
with this right thumb
sky always always shone in them.

CROSSING

Marram whipped, peat-lipped,
salt-scoured, windswept:
the earth meets the sea

and each opens to the running sky
and reflects it. Gazing across
the wash of years

we say this stark foreshore
where flux is the only constant
looks entirely fitting

as the site of a crossing-place
and while we recognise
it's not what its makers intended

with their plans for circles and walkways
well-guarded by dunes,
and their heroic labour,

see also that time and dream
have mapped and remapped it
into another truth.

TIDES

Of what once was
what's left will soon be gone.

Without kicking up more waves
of argument and speculation,

or putting unanswerable
philosophical questions...

Still not knowing how not to look,
and not to ask but breathe

and have my own tides reveal
what they will and when they will.

Wrynecks drum, grey plovers whistle,
and boring piddocks have their way.

Of what once was
what's left will soon be gone.

Wholly to immerse myself
wholly to find myself.

Not to search for words words
but in this place only to be.

BURDEN

Not sorry and not stricken
but of age
I'll strip my scape
to headland
            and heartland.

Let each silence
            and breath
each word-in-waiting
learn to bear a burden
weightless as eternity.

AFTERWORD

The existence of a timber circle not far from Holme and Old Hunstanton in North Norfolk, already known to archaeologists, was the subject of great interest and excitement when the press picked it up in January 1999. I covered it for the BBC World Service – one of 32 well-clad people who converged on it as daylight broke on a freezing, blustery morning – and had to burrow into a sand dune to get adequate protection for my microphone.

The circle, standing on the foreshore and regularly covered by the incoming tides, consisted of 55 split oak trunks. It measured just over 20ft across, and at the centre was a huge oak stump, upside down.

It is now generally agreed that this circle, known as Seahenge, was constructed in the Early Bronze Age by semi-nomadic Beaker Folk (originally from Spain) who were settling along the coast of eastern and southern Britain. Much more specifically,

HOLME I – 'SEAHENGE' 2049BC - 1999AD

and quite remarkably, dendrochronology and carbon-B dating prove that the oak trees used for the circle were all felled in spring or summer 2049BC.

At least 50 bronze axes (two or more of which have been found) were used during the felling, and the timbers were dragged into position by people using honeysuckle ropes. Archaeologists also agree that the site of the circle was originally maybe one-and-a-half miles or so inland, probably on a saltmarsh – and that it was one of a complex including at least one other circle and pathways and causeways.

Recently, at low water during the very lowest of neap tides, Andy Rafferty has been able to photograph eight upright oak trunks that are plainly part of a second circle.

So what were these circles? As ever we have to use what archaeological evidence we can, and then imagine. A place

HOLME II 2049BC

where body and spirit meet. A mortuary perhaps? A site for sky-burials?

In my sequence of poems, my journey begins where I grew up, under Whiteleaf Cross in the Chiltern Hills. The shed at the top of our garden became my childhood museum, and there I exhibited my finds – pieces of Iron Age pottery, fossils from the chalkpit, and a Roman coin. Neighbours began to visit the museum, and generously to add to my collection. After following the Neolithic Icknield Way and Peddars Way that plays out into the sea at Holme, I then adopt the persona of a woman who helps to build the timber circle of Seahenge and lay the body of her father within it.

Whiteleaf. . . and North Norfolk. . . my headland, my heartland.

Kevin Crossley-Holland

IMAGES

All the images in *Seahenge: A Journey* are single-frame photographs, not composites, taken at a moment in time – albeit that a 'moment' may range from a fraction of a second to several seconds. Many images are the result of intentional camera movement performed during the opening of the shutter, some are the result of subject movement and some are a combination of camera movement and subject movement. Post-production adjustments have been kept to a minimum.

The images are my response to the poem sequence and were taken along the Icknield Way and Peddars Way, (notwithstanding the occasional detour), but readers should feel free to attach a location, an impression, a moment in time from their own experience, memory or emotion that chimes with the poem sequence. That said, for the curious, the locations of my images are given overleaf.

Andrew Rafferty

IMAGE LOCATIONS

Front cover: Holme-next-the-Sea
Back cover: Covehithe

1. Whiteleaf Hill barrow, Buckinghamshire
2. KCH museum collection
3. Five Knolls, Icknield Way, Bedfordshire
4. Woodwalton Fen, Cambridgeshire
5. King's Forest, Suffolk
6. Harpley Common barrow, Norfolk
7. Cley Marsh, Norfolk
8. Sedgeford Belt, Ringstead, Norfolk
9. Above Whiteleaf, Buckinghamshire
10. 'Mommet', Great Bircham, Norfolk
11. Bird Hill, Clothall, Hertfordshire
12. Saltings, Holme-next-the-Sea, Norfolk
13. River Hun, Holme-next-the-Sea, Norfolk
14. Honeypot Wood, East Dereham, Norfolk
15. Easton Broad, Covehithe, Suffolk
16. Beacon Hill, Thornham, Norfolk
17. Above Bunker's Wood bowl-barrow, Norfolk
18. Easton Broad, Covehithe, Suffolk
19. Musk Mallow, Harpley Common barrow
20. River Gade, Great Gaddesdon, Hertfordshire
21. Whiteleaf, Buckinghamshire
22. Holme-next-the-Sea, Norfolk
23. Holme-next-the-Sea, Norfolk
24. Holme-next-the-Sea, Norfolk
25. Holme-next-the-Sea, Norfolk
26. Holme-next-the-Sea, Norfolk
27. Holme I (Seahenge), Norfolk, just before its removal
28. Holme II, West Sands, Holme-next-the-Sea